INTRODUCT

I came to work in Birmingham in the early 1950s, a time when the city was being torn apart by massive post-war developments. It was some twenty years before I began to appreciate that it was not simply an immense building site but had become an attractive twentieth century city, still, however, retaining many reminders of its distinguished past.

Birmingham is a busy place to which people come to earn their living and not, primarily, for sight-seeing. But there is a great deal more than employment to be found in its busy streets. Much of Britain's industrial and commercial history is linked with the region, for it was in the West Midlands that the Industrial Revolution had its beginnings – a revolution that not only physically transformed the region but also transformed the lives of everyone in the British Isles. If you have time to stand and stare not only will you discover many links with that past but you will also find much of cultural and architectural interest.

In this book I take you on a guided tour of part of this great city. I have attempted to present a picture of Birmingham as it is today and to show how much of its past can still be discovered in its streets and buildings. The complete walk covers about 4½ miles though this can be reduced to 4 miles if you omit two short excursions from the canal section. The amount of time taken to complete it will depend very much on how long you allow for studying the features that I have highlighted: if you keep this to a minimum you can get around in about half a day. But if you want to go into museums and cathedrals and notable buildings you could easily spend a day or more.

The walk begins and ends at Victoria Square. However, as it is a circular walk you do not necessarily need to start there but can join wherever is most convenient.

A problem with describing a walk through a city is that changes can take place quite rapidly and, sometimes, unexpectedly. I hope that all the features I have described will be here for many years, but obviously there can be no guarantee that will be the case.

The strip maps throughout the book should help you to keep to the route and to locate the features that I describe. Please be careful on the roads and always use pedestrian crossings and underpasses, with which the city is well endowed. A pair of binoculars would be useful if you want to study architectural details.

Peter Groves
March 1987.

N
Snow Hill
Snow Hill Arch
Livery Street
Ludgate Hill
Charlotte Street
45
44
Newhall Street
43
42
Saturday Bridge
46
47
48
Tindal Bridge
49
Birmingham Canal
51
52
Broad Street
Gas Street
50
53
54
55
56
57
58
59
60
61
62
63
Chamberlain Square
Paradise Street
Hill Street
3
2
1
14
15
Margaret Street
Cornwall St.
17
16
Edmund Street
Newhall Street
18
19
13
12
Waterloo
11
START
4
New Street

Exploring Birmingham

A guided tour by Peter Groves

ACKNOWLEDGEMENTS

In the preparation of this book I have benefitted from valuable discussions with a number of people and I would particularly like to thank the following for their help:

George Ball, Mike Benson, Douglas Hickman, Doreen and Peter Price, Stephen Price.

I am also greatly appreciative of the help of my wife Jean who has carefully read the typescript, walked the route with me, and made many valuable comments and suggestions.

I am grateful to the following for permission to reproduce some of the photographs in this book:

G Schienke (page 11); Reference Library, Local Studies Department, Birmingham Public Libraries (pages 20, 23, 26, 34); Birmingham City Museum and Art Gallery (page 37). The print on page 24 was kindly supplied by Lewis's Ltd.

Notes added January 1989

Since this book was first printed there have, inevitably, been new building developments in Birmingham. The principal changes have been in Broad Street where the new International Conference Centre is being constructed. This has not significantly affected this walk although, with the reconstruction of Paradise Circus, it will soon be possible to walk straight across from the Hall of Memory to the Library complex (page 49) without having to use an underpass.

The Broad Street tunnel (page 42) has now diminished in extent as a result of the Conference Centre developments. If, as a result of further work, you find the tunnel closed, return to Tindal Bridge, cross this and walk up Cambridge Street until you reach the rear of the Repertory Theatre. Turn right beside the theatre and you will come out onto Broad Street. You can then either pick up the route from here (page 45) or else walk along Broad Street to Gas Street, go down this road to Gas Street Basin and rejoin the route there.

The Birmingham Brasshouse (page 44), after decaying for several years, has now been converted into an attractive restaurant.

Various changes are planned for the Bull Ring area (page 11) although this is peripheral to *Exploring Birmingham*. It seems possible that the Rotunda may disappear.

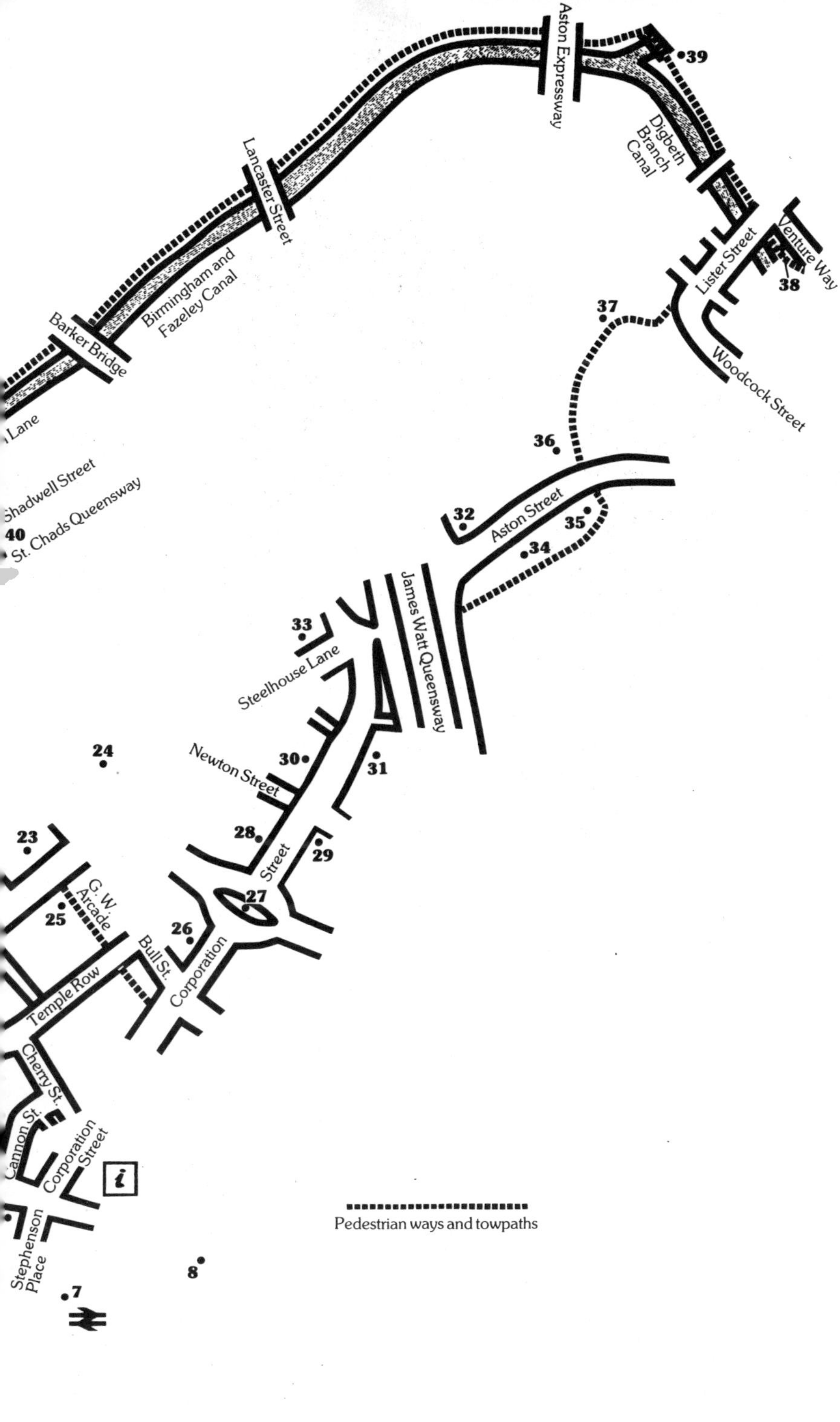
Aston Expressway
39
Digbeth Branch Canal
Lancaster Street
Birmingham and Fazeley Canal
Barker Bridge
Lister Street
Venture Way
38
37
Woodcock Street
Lane
Shadwell Street
St. Chads Queensway
40
36
Aston Street
32
35
34
James Watt Queensway
33
Steelhouse Lane
24
Newton Street
30
31
28
29
Street
23
G.W. Arcade
27
25
26
Bull St.
Corporation
Temple Row
Cherry St.
Cannon St.
Corporation Street
i
Stephenson Place
8
7
Pedestrian ways and towpaths

Exploring Birmingham

We start our walk in Victoria Square, the heart of nineteenth century Birmingham and the scene of rallies and public events and meetings. Today it provides an attractive paved and grassed area where you can sit and watch the activity of a busy city flow around you. Birmingham's city centre is remarkably compact and contains few open spaces, but this area was opened out in 1972 by the demolition of a number of old buildings. The statue of Queen Victoria was unveiled by Princess Margaret in 1951 and is a recasting in bronze of an earlier one erected in 1901.

From Victoria Square you can see a number of notable buildings. Most prominent is the Renaissance style **Council House (1),** opened in 1879. It is ornamented with a variety of sculptures, and the gable over the main entrance shows Britannia crowning Birmingham's manufacturers with laurel wreaths. Beneath this is an attractive Venetian mosaic.

The Council House was built when Birmingham was at the peak of its power as 'the workshop of the world'. The Mayor, Joseph Chamberlain, was a man of great vision and drive and was determined to put Birmingham in the forefront of municipal progress. He entered the Council in 1868 and when he left in 1883 for national politics he could claim that the town had been 'parked, paved, assized, marketed, gas-and-watered, and improved'. His reforms became world famous and he has been justly venerated by Birmingham citizens. In 1890 an American observer described Birmingham as 'the best-governed city in the world'. Birmingham acquired city status in 1889, the coat of arms being based on the crest of the de Bermingham family, lords of the Manor of Birmingham from the twelfth to the sixteenth century.

The foundation stone of the Council House was laid by Joseph Chamberlain in 1874. You will find this near the left-hand corner of the building.

To the west of Victoria Square is the **Town Hall (2).** This impressive building, made from Anglesey marble, now appreciably weathered, is a copy of the Temple of Castor and Pollux in the Roman Forum, and stands on an arched platform of large roughly cut stones. The architects, J A Hansom (better known

◄ **The Council House**

for the Hansom cab) and E Welch, won an open competition with this design in 1830. Unfortunately, they were required to stand surety for the building and, following serious financial problems over the construction, were declared bankrupt in 1834, two years after work had started. However, although it had not been completed, the Hall was opened in that year and a music festival was held. A local architect, Charles Edge, continued to supervise the construction but the Hall was not finished until about the middle of the century.

The first contested parliamentary election for Birmingham's two MPs was held in the Town Hall in 1835, the Reform Act of 1832 having granted the franchise to the town. The election proved so lively that the front of the gallery collapsed under the pressure of the crowd!

But these were troubled times, and in 1839 the Town Hall was used as the headquarters of a 2,000 strong force of special constabulary. The Chartist movement, which advocated parliamentary reform, was especially powerful in Birmingham but had been split between those who favoured peaceful methods and those who advocated violent means to achieve their aims. In 1839 the revolutionary leaders were in the ascendancy. In July, riots broke out in the Bull Ring but were soon quelled by the police and soldiers. Almost all of the Chartist's aims, including universal manhood suffrage and voting by ballot, were, nevertheless, achieved peacefully over the next eighty years.

In December 1901 the Town Hall was the scene of another lively incident. The future Prime Minister, David Lloyd George, then a young Liberal MP who

The Town Hall

opposed Britain's involvement in the Boer War, was prevented from speaking there by his political opponents who set up such a clamour of yelling, stamping and whistling that not a word of his speech could be heard. Then a mob outside started hurling stones through the windows and in the ensuing mêlée Lloyd George escaped only by exchanging clothes with a policeman and marching out of the Hall as part of a police squad.

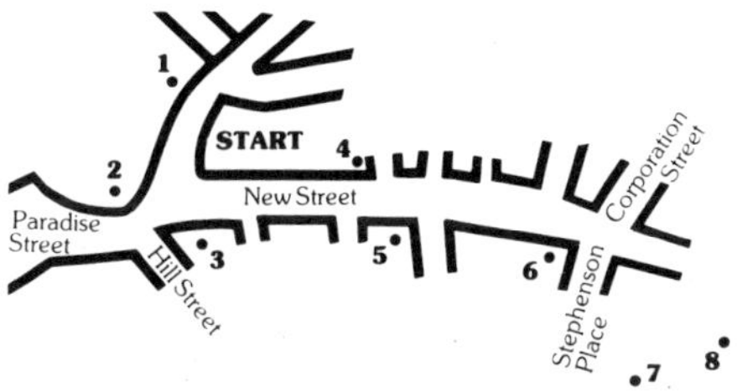

The Town Hall has played a distinguished part in Birmingham's musical history. Mendelssohn played on the magnificent organ, the pipes of which still retain their original decoration. Two notable first performances here were of Mendelssohn's Elijah in 1846 and Elgar's Dream of Gerontius in 1900. Today it is the home of the City of Birmingham Symphony Orchestra, a fine orchestra with an international reputation. The interior of the Hall was altered in 1926 when an opulent new ceiling was fitted and an additional gallery built to increase the seating. Each Wednesday lunchtime there is a free public organ recital.

We shall return to Victoria Square later but now walk across the Square and over the pedestrian crossing to New Street on the corner of which stands the **General Post Office (3).** Opened to the public in 1890, this building was described at the time as 'coarse and commonplace'. However, a few years ago, plans by the Post Office to demolish the building had to be abandoned in the face of determined local opposition. An adjacent building, belonging to the Post Office, was demolished and on the site is now an attractive office block (No. 1 Victoria Square) opened in 1985 and designed to stand comfortably alongside the Town Hall, the Council House and the other distinguished buildings nearby.

In spite of its name, New Street is one of the oldest streets in Birmingham and it is known to have existed in the fourteenth century. Much of New Street is still Victorian, in a variety of architectural styles. Turn left as you face the Post Office and walk down on the right-hand side of New Street.

No. 56, **Grosvenor House (4),** on the corner of Bennett's Hill, is of interest as the first post-war building in the city centre, having been completed in 1953. This site was redeveloped by the property magnate Jack Cotton who was responsible for much of the constructional work in the city in the early sixties. The ornamented style of this building was an attempt to make it blend in with the surrounding buildings.

The **Piccadilly Arcade (5),** which you pass on your right, was originally built as the Picture House, the first of Birmingham's cinemas. The Picture House was opened in 1910 and closed in 1926 when it was converted into the present arcade. The arcade still retains some of its original shopfronts and, at the far end, a fine brass handrail. Its origin as a cinema makes sense of the sloping floor where the auditorium was presumably situated.

On the corner of Stephenson Place is the old **Midland Bank (6),** an

Queen's Corner. The junction of New Street and Corporation Street

attractive building in the classical style dating from 1869. On the opposite corner, and in stark contrast, is the modern Midland Bank opened in 1972.

Stephenson Place gives pedestrian access to **New Street Station (7),** Birmingham's principal railway station. The city's first station was opened in Curzon Street in 1837, the line to Euston being constructed by George Stephenson and his son Robert. However, Curzon Street proved inadequate for the immense demand for rail transport and, although the building fortunately still exists, it was replaced in 1854 by a new station in New Street. This was connected to the existing railway lines by tunnels under the city centre. When it was opened the Birmingham Gazette commented that 'the vast structure merits the distinction of being the finest railway station in the world'. This, however, was not a popular sentiment; Birmingham's other main line station, Snow Hill, was always much more highly regarded until it closed in 1972.

Like the canals before them, the railways made a major contribution to the prosperity of the region. They provided a cheaper and faster means of transporting raw materials and finished goods than either the roads or the canals. The increase in prosperity was paralleled by a growth in population which in the middle years of the nineteenth century more than doubled from 144,000 in 1831 to 344,000 in 1871.

New Street station was enlarged in 1880 and then completely reconstructed in the 1960s, being officially reopened in March 1967. The track and twelve platforms are below ground level and they cater for about 600 trains and 50-60,000 passengers a day. Above is a massive concrete slab covering 7.5 acres and supported by more than 200 columns. It carries a shopping precinct (the Pallasades), containing over a hundred shops, which is linked by a covered pedestrian way to another shopping precinct, the Bull Ring Centre. From New Street station there are through trains to more towns, as far apart as Inverness and Penzance, than from any other British Rail station.

Opposite Stephenson Place, on the

other side of New Street, is Corporation Street. This street was built in the 1870s and 1880s as part of Joseph Chamberlain's plan for the development and improvement of the city. His intention was to construct 'a great street, broad as a Parisian boulevard, from New Street to the Aston Road'. Its construction involved the redevelopment of a mean and unhealthy slum area renowned for crime and wretchedness.

Post-war building developments have brought many changes to Corporation Street and the construction of the pedestrian underpass at Bull Street(which you will meet later) has broken the continuity of the street. However, many buildings dating from Chamberlain's day remain.

If you look up to the top of the building at the left-hand junction of New Street and Corporation Street you will see the inscription "Queen's Corner", a name which today seems to have fallen into disuse. It commemorates the visit of Queen Victoria to Birmingham in 1887.

Cross to Queen's Corner at the pedestrian crossing and look down to the lower end of New Street. Prominent there is the **Rotunda (8),** its high circular tower being one of Birmingham's most prominent landmarks. It was opened in 1965 and stands on high ground overlooking the city's famous Bull Ring.

The Bull Ring is the site of Birmingham's medieval village green, but it is too much off our route to include here. It is,

The Rotunda at night G Schienke

however, well worth a subsequent visit. The Bull Ring area, which contains an open market, was much damaged in the second world war and today is most notable for St. Martin's Church, the city's Parish Church built in 1873 on the site of the earlier thirteenth century church. The east and west windows are products of the world-famous and still active Birmingham stained glass firm of Hardman's Studios, who also designed and made the windows in the Houses of Parliament.

Now start back up New Street and almost immediately turn right up Cannon Street. There are a number of Victorian buildings here, the most interesting being No. 36, **Norfolk House (9),** its doorway flanked by the smiling faces of two jesters, and No. 17 which is particularly attractive. Then turn left into the pedestrianised Cherry Street, originally a footpath across a cherry orchard. This will bring you to Temple Row where Birmingham Cathedral faces you. Although much of the churchyard has been paved and is widely used as a concourse, a number of old tombs remain. Just ahead you will find a memorial to John Heap and William Badger who were both killed in an accident in 1833 when a pulley block failed during the building of the Town Hall. The memorial is the base of a pillar which had been carved by one of them for the Hall.

We shall return to the Cathedral later but now turn left and walk along Temple Row, immediately passing on your left the impressive and powerful 1980s Bank of England building. On the corner of **Waterloo Street (10)** is a fine late Gothic building in brick and terracotta with, high up, a frieze containing roses, thistles and shamrocks. This was built in 1900 for

Ocean Assurance on a site originally occupied by the Freehold Land Society, a forerunner of today's building societies. This society amalgamated in 1900 with several others to form the Birmingham Incorporated Building Society, now the Birmingham Midshires Building Society. If you look over the entrance you will see more roses, thistles and shamrocks, and also a repeated pattern of the letters O and A (for Ocean Assurance).

This building has recently been modernised and extended, the extension in Waterloo Street blending in nicely with the older part. The leaded windows of the old building presented the architects with considerable difficulties during the modernisation as they were protected by a preservation order. They became the first windows ever to incorporate leaded double glazing.

Waterloo Street was so named to celebrate the victory over Napoleon in 1815. Continue along this street to the junction with Bennett's Hill where you will find two important Victorian banks. First is the Midland Bank, a bold and impressive 1830 building. Across Bennett's Hill is the **National Westminster Bank (11),** built in 1869 as the National Provincial Bank and surmounted by a superb coat of arms (based on the city's arms) which is screened by a wire mesh to protect it from the corrosive droppings of starlings which, at sunset, flock into the city in their thousands to roost. The building magnificently symbolises the prestige and confidence of the Victorian banking system. The semi-domed entrance porch has a fine ceiling and four sculpted panels representing Birmingham industry. You will see the sculptor's name and the date inscribed on the panels.

Bennett's Hill, named after the family who originally farmed here, was laid out in 1827. Some of the original buildings remain in the upper end (to the right), including a terrace of five houses (Nos. 1-5) and a detached house (No. 6). The buildings opposite these, including The Wellington public house, date from later in the century and are particularly attractive.

The painter Edward Burne-Jones was born in Bennett's Hill and if you would like to make a short excursion down the hill you will find a plaque recording this fact about half-way down, on the Royal Bank of Scotland building on the right.

Now continue along Waterloo Street, carefully crossing to the right-hand side of the street. Look across for a further view of the National Provincial Bank.

The area around Waterloo Street was improved in the early part of the nineteenth century and became the main commercial sector of the city. Many of the very attractive buildings date from this period. **Waterloo Court (12)** (36 Waterloo Street) is particularly interesting, its Corinthian columns being copied from the Tower of the Winds in Athens. It was altered in 1976 and the frontage now provides access to a pleasant courtyard. Apsley House, next door, is another fine building.

Continue along Waterloo Street and then turn right into Colmore Row. This

The entrance porch to the National Westminster Bank

is named after the Colmore family who acquired their fortune in the sixteenth century and subsequently played an important part in Birmingham's history. They lived in New Hall, leading to which was a great avenue of elm trees, now Newhall Street (which you will meet later in this walk).

This part of Colmore Row was originally known as Ann Street (named after a member of the Colmore family) and was rebuilt from 1866 onwards, the old poor buildings being replaced by more prestigious structures, many of which still exist.

Walk along Colmore Row. Particularly notable among the Victorian buildings that you pass is the **Bank of Scotland (13).** This was originally constructed for the Eagle Life Insurance Company in 1900 and has been described by Nicholas Pevsner, the great authority on the buildings of England, as 'one of the most original buildings of its date in England'. The interior is charming, and the round headed doorway and bronze doors are particularly interesting. The parapet, supported on alternate parabolic and triangular arches, carries

Waterloo Street

the carving of an eagle – but you will not be able to see this until you have crossed the road a little further on.

On the opposite side of the road you will see two impressive modern banks (Lloyds, and the 250ft. high National Westminster). At the pedestrian crossing (just past the National Westminster) cross the street and then turn left to walk back along Colmore Row. Note the buildings across the street, especially No. 110 Colmore Row, built for the Scottish Union and National Assurance Company, with its attractive banded frontage; and remember to look up to the parapet of the Bank of Scotland.

Continue forward to the Council House, then turn right at the far end of this and you will find yourself in Chamberlain Square. On your right, and forming part of the Council House building, is the **City Museum and Art Gallery (14).** This was opened in 1885 by the Prince of Wales (later to become King Edward VII), its main acquisitions having been donated by Thomas Osler. Osler was a local glassmaker whose firm constructed a greatly admired glass fountain, the centrepiece of the Great Exhibition of 1851. He initiated a fund, the Public Picture Gallery Fund, which has provided many important acquisitions for the Gallery.

The memorial stone in the entrance hall carries the words 'By the gains of industry we promote Art'. This is a fitting reminder of the fact that the Gallery was largely paid for from the profits of the Municipal Gas Company, one example of Joseph Chamberlain's highly successful municipal enterprises.

The Art Gallery is renowned for its collection of Pre-Raphaelite paintings and contains masterpieces of Ford Madox Brown, Edward Burne-Jones, Holman Hunt, John Millais and Dante Gabriel Rossetti. The Pre-Raphaelite movement was founded in 1848 by Rossetti, Holman Hunt and Millais and had, as its philosophy, a wish to return to pre-Renaissance ideals. Its works have a great minuteness of detail and a brilliance of colour.

A prominent feature in Chamberlain Square is 'Big Brum', the clock tower at the north-western corner of the Art Gallery and, perhaps, Birmingham's answer to 'Big Ben'.

At the end of the first World War an extension to the Gallery was opened, the Feeney Galleries, funds for which

Big Brum

were provided from the will of a local benefactor, John Feeney. The extension also included the Natural History Museum which was opened in 1913. One of the aims of this Museum was 'to enable the citizen to take an intelligent interest in the various forms of animal and vegetable life that he may come across in his occasional walks beyond the limits of city streets, and to stimulate the imagination by showing the wonderful diversity of natural life of the earth...' The diversity of natural life is superbly illustrated by the collection which ranges from local to far-away places, from existing creatures to those long extinct, including an ever-popular life-size model of a dinosaur. The Museum also includes extensive geological, archaeological and coin collections. In recent years a local history section has been added, the entrance to which is at the rear of the complex in Great Charles Street.

Now continue past the main Museum and Art Gallery entrance and turn right to pass under a bridge, dated 1885 and 1911, which links the Art Gallery to the **Council House Extension (15)** on your left. This Edwardian renaissance building was constructed between 1910 and 1919 and is in Darley Dale stone to match the Council House.

You will now find yourself in a quiet and peaceful oasis away from the bustle of the surrounding city. Central to this part of Chamberlain Square is a statue of George Dawson, a radical reformer who was influential in promoting governmental and municipal social legislation. He was a member of the Executive of the National Education League founded in 1898, a political body centred in Birmingham which worked vigorously for local authorities to be compelled to provide free education for all children in their district.

Around the Dawson statue is a fine set of wrought iron gates manufactured in the late nineteenth century which originally stood at the entrance to the old Reference Library. Nearby you will see a reminder of an earlier form of public transport, a length of tram lines.

The first tramway was built in Birmingham in 1873 and ran between Colmore Row and Hockley. It was constructed by the Council and was leased to a private company, the Birmingham and District Tramway Company. The cars were pulled by horses. More tramway companies were established, the Council providing the track and the companies using the lines on lease. Horses were soon replaced by steam but the steam cars were considered 'hideous, cumbrous and dangerous'. After experimenting with a cable driven system between Colmore Row and the bottom of Hockley Hill, battery driven electric cars were introduced along the Bristol Road. However, these proved a failure, frequently running out of power and leaving the passengers stranded. Eventually, on 1 January 1907 and after bitter arguments about the relative merits of overhead and surface powered systems, the city was converted to electric tramways using overhead wires. A Government Bill of 1903 enabled the Council to take over the tramway companies and by 1911 these were all in municipal ownership, profits from the system soon contributing handsomely to the relief of rates and to improving the conditions of municipal employees. The first motor buses were purchased in 1913 and these gradually replaced the trams, the last of which ran in 1953. An old city tram is preserved in the Museum of Science and Industry which we shall meet later.

Walk along Chamberlain Square into Margaret Street where there are two particularly interesting buildings. Almost opposite is the original building for the **Birmingham School of Art and Crafts (16),** built in the 1880s and now part of the Faculty of Art and Design of Birmingham Polytechnic. It is decorated with a lively array of Gothic gables, panels and windows, and with mosaics and decorated tiles. Note, high up, the remarkable round panel with a trellis-work pattern entwined with lilies. The building was a late work of the Birmingham architect, J H Chamberlain (no relation of Joseph Chamberlain), who designed many of the city's schools and the Chamberlain Memorial Fountain in Chamberlain Square (which you will meet later).

On the far corner of Cornwall Street is the **Birmingham and Midland Institute (17).** The Institute was founded by Act of Parliament in 1854 and occupied a site adjacent to the Town Hall from 1857 until 1965 when the building was demolished. The Institute then moved to the present building which had been the home of the Birmingham Library, a private subscription library founded in 1779.

The Institute was a pioneer of advanced education in Birmingham – scientific and technical for the benefit of local industry, and non-vocational to encourage education in general. One of its supporters was Charles Dickens who, in 1853, gave readings of *The Chimes* and *A Christmas Carol* in the Town Hall

George Dawson

to raise funds to establish the Institute. Dickens was elected sixteenth President of the Institute in 1869.

The Institute now provides club facilities to its members and is the home of affiliated societies which cater for a wide range of leisure activities.

Now walk along Cornwall Street. At the side entrance to the Birmingham and Midland Institute, just before No. 95, you will find the original foundation stone to the Institute, laid by Prince Albert in 1855 and moved to its present position in 1974.

The brick and stone houses on your left date from the turn of the century and are all attractive, especially No. 85-87 with its two balconies. Turn right into Newhall Street (no trace now of the magnificent elms!). As you walk up this street you will see, on the left, the red brick Scottish Mutual Assurance office, built in 1895, which carries three iron railed balconies. A little further on is a richly ornamented brick and terracotta building fronted with a striking set of iron gates. This is the old **Telephone House (18)** dating from 1896. The first Birmingham telephone exchange was opened with twelve subscribers in 1879. The present Telephone House is lower down Newhall Street and was opened in 1969.

Carry on up Newhall Street until you find yourself back in Colmore Row. Carefully cross at the pedestrian crossing and then turn left to walk along Colmore Row, observing as you do the fine Victorian buildings on the opposite side. **No. 85 Colmore Row (19),** now the offices of the Woolwich Building Society, is a particularly attractive piece of architecture. It was built as the Union Club, and was a popular meeting place for Victorian businessmen.

Benvenuto Cellini in Colmore Row

Set high up in No. 81, now the **National and Provincial Building Society (20),** are roundels containing busts of Lorenzo Ghiberti and Benvenuto Cellini. Ghiberti (1378-1455) was a Florentine sculptor in metal; Cellini (1500-1571) was perhaps the most famous goldsmith of all time and was born and trained in Florence. The relevance of these characters to Colmore Row becomes clear when it is realised that the property was built in 1871-73 for Mr W Spurrier, a Birmingham silversmith and cutler. The design of the roundels is similar to a series of *Heads of the Prophets* in one of Ghiberti's most renowned works, the *Gates of Paradise* at the East Door of the Baptistry in Florence.

A little further along is Barclays Bank, 63 Colmore Row, built in 1867, the facade being remodelled in 1937. However, the banking hall remains in all its Victorian glory.

You now have a good view ahead, across Temple Row West, of the Cathedral. But first go right a little way along Temple Row West to view several interesting buildings on the right including **Lloyds Bank (21).** This was built in 1862-64, the architect being J A

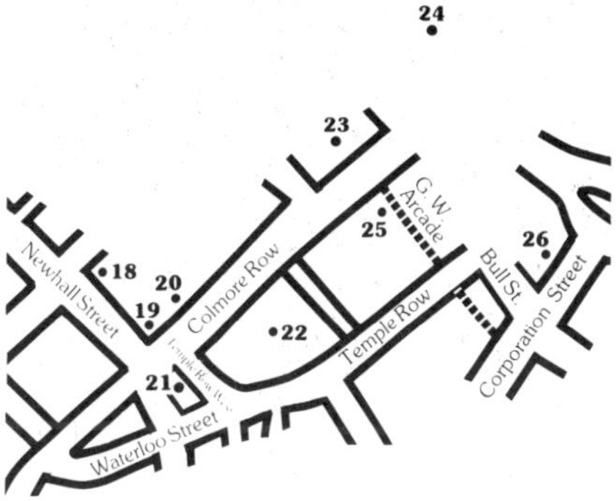

Chatwin who was well known for his Gothic churches. The ground floor contains a magnificent Victorian banking hall, somewhat spoiled by the more recent addition of wooden partitioning.

Cross Temple Row West to the churchyard of St. Philip's and walk across this to the entrance to **Birmingham Cathedral (22).** The parish of Birmingham was created by Act of Parliament in 1708 and the parish church, St. Philip's, was built mainly between 1709 and 1715. It was, at that time, surrounded by fields and orchards. The tower and dome were completed in 1725, George I having contributed £600 to the costs. This gift was at the suggestion of Sir Richard Gough and is recorded in the entrance to the church by the following acknowledgement:

> His most Excellent Majesty King George I upon the kind Application of Sr. Richard Gough to the Rt. Honourable Sr. Rob. Walpole Gave £600 towards finishing this CHURCH AD1725.

If you look up at the weather vane on the tower you will see that it carries a boar's head instead of the traditional cock. This was a gesture to the Gough family whose crest included a boar's head.

Charles Gore, first Bishop of Birmingham

On one side of the entrance is an imposing bronze statue of Charles Gore, first Bishop of Birmingham, 1905-11. Nearby, on the other side of the entrance, you can find the smallest stone in the churchyard. This is in memory of Nanetta Stocker who died in 1819. According to the stone she was

> 'the smallest woman ever in this Kingdom, possessed with every accomplishment. Only 33 inches high. Native of Austria.'

The stone is just 33 inches long.

The dedication of the church to St. Philip was not the result of any particular attachment to this saint, merely that the plot on which the church was built had been sold to the church commissioners by Mrs Elizabeth Philips. The architect was a local gentleman, Thomas Archer, and the builder one William Shakespeare. Thomas Archer had travelled widely on the continent and his design ('English Baroque') was considerably influenced by the Italian architect Borromini as well as by English architects including Sir Christopher Wren. St. Philip's Church became Birmingham Cathedral in 1905.

The interior is beautifully plastered and gilded. Of particular interest are the four magnificent stained glass windows dating from the 1880s and 1890s which seem to glow from their own light. They are *The Nativity, The Crucifixion, The Ascension* and *The Last Judgement* and were designed by Sir Edward Burne-Jones (born in 1833 and christened in St. Philip's) and made by William Morris. Note the fine panelled fronts of the galleries and the magnificent organ. The cross in gold, silver and crystal is a beautiful modern work and was presented after the war by the Friends of the Cathedral. At the head of the south aisle there is a modern embroidered panel representing God's creative energy. In front of this is the font made in phosphor bronze in 1982. Opposite, in the north aisle, is a sculpture of Christ crucified made from copper on wood which was dedicated in 1984.

Now continue along Colmore Row, noting that the grass verges that fringe the churchyard are edged with the granite setts which originally paved the

◄ **Birmingham Cathedral**

Birmingham Public Libraries

The Cathedral weather vane

city streets. On the opposite side is the Grand Hotel, an opulent piece of Victorian Renaissance. Just beyond this is the **Sun Alliance building (23),** opened in 1985, a delighful glass fronted structure (though not to everyone's taste) with a conservatory-like entrance hall. It is on the site of the old Snow Hill station which was opened in 1852 (two years before New Street station) and from which the last train ran on 6 March 1972. The Great Western Railway line between Snow Hill and Paddington was built by Brunel between 1847 and 1852. A new Snow Hill station (1987) will now take local trains which originally terminated at Moor Street.

If you look across to the north-east you

will see **Birmingham Post and Mail House (24).** Opened in 1965, this grey glass and aluminium fronted block seemed to mark a turning point for Birmingham architecture. Until then much post-war building had been dull or, sometimes, ugly. But since 1965 some fine buildings have been erected which are more appropriate to the city's status.

The Post and Mail House is designed in keeping with the natural flow of newspaper production. Editorial and advertising material flows downwards in the building. Production flows upwards, from the printing presses in the lowest of five basements to the despatch department on the ground floor. The presses consume some 180,000 miles of paper and 300 tonnes of ink per year. Computer technology is extensively employed by the journalists and by the editorial and design staff.

Birmingham's first newspaper was Aris's Birmingham Gazette, first published in 1741 by Thomas Aris and printed on a hand press in New Street. Another newspaper, the Birmingham Journal, appeared in 1825, being published by a group of Tories who had objected to remarks appearing about them in the London Times. The Birmingham Journal was a predecessor to the Birmingham Post which first appeared as a daily paper in 1858. The Gazette was merged with the Post in 1956. The Post's sister paper, the Birmingham Evening Mail was first published, as a halfpenny paper, in 1870.

Now turn right, opposite the Sun Alliance, into the **Great Western Arcade (25).** This prestigious Victorian arcade, built over a railway tunnel in 1876, has two storeys with shops on the ground floor and a first floor gallery. The original glass roof was,

The entrance to the Sun Alliance building

unfortunately, destroyed in the Second World War. A plaque, a few yards inside the entrance on the left, records the re-opening of the restored arcade by the Lord Mayor in 1984. When you have entered the main part of the arcade look back and up to the attractive clock with five hanging bells which ring out the Westminster chimes. Although this was only installed in 1984 and has a modern mechanism the bells were cast in the traditional way at the Whitechapel Bell Foundry, Britain's oldest bell foundry dating back to the fourteenth century. This was the birthplace of many distinguished bells, including Big Ben.

As you leave the Great Western Arcade at Temple Row look up at the entrance arch to a sculpture representing the city's arts and sciences.

Cross Temple Row into the North Western Arcade. The original arcade has been demolished and this dates from 1957 when the adjacent shops were built. On the right is Rackhams, one of Birmingham's largest stores.

When you emerge into Corporation Street turn left and immediately descend to the pedestrian underpass which will take you into a busy shopping area below street level. Carry on forward and then ascend to street level. This will bring you out alongside **Lewis's (26),** another of Birmingham's major stores. Joseph Chamberlain was anxious to see that Corporation Street became a prestigious shopping centre and he invited David Lewis, who already had several successful stores in the North of England, to come here. Lewis was somewhat dubious at first but did open a tea shop in New Street in 1882. He then carried out his own market research and observed that the part of the city centre which had the greatest flow of shoppers was the junction of Bull Street and Corporation Street. The original store was opened on this site in 1885. In the 1920s adjacent shops were bought up and the present building was constructed. In 1929 a second block was erected on an adjacent site in Bull Street and connected to the first by two bridges across a public thoroughfare, The Minories. The link was further extended in the 1970s.

The Great Western Arcade in 1876

Birmingham Public Libraries

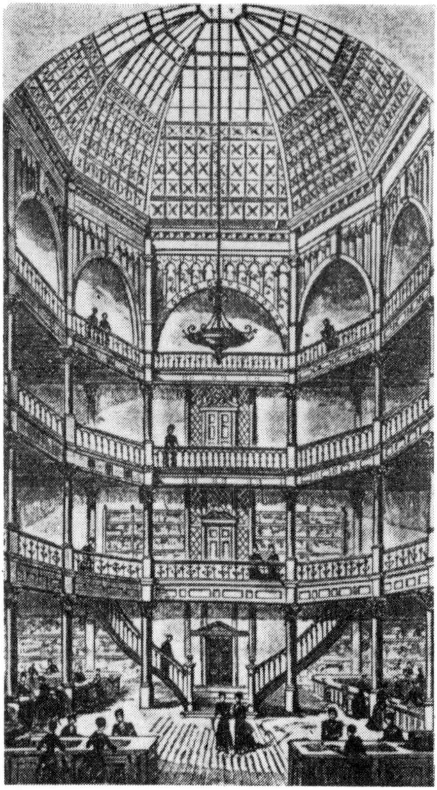

Lewis's Store in 1885

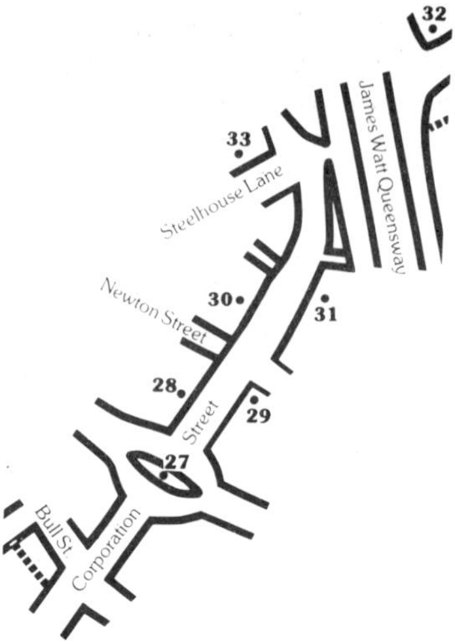

Beyond Lewis's descend the underpass to another shopping area. This is on the site of Birmingham's **Old Square (27)** which, in the eighteenth century, had been occupied by well-to-do merchants and professional men. There were many fine houses with large gardens and views over the countryside. Nothing of these remains today, although the city has installed a fine plaque, recording something of the history and residents of the Square, which you will see on your left as you walk forward. One resident was Sampson Lloyd who in 1765, with John Taylor, established Taylors and Lloyds Bank in nearby Dale End. After Taylor had withdrawn from the business this became the first Lloyds Bank.

Now go through the underpass ahead and turn right to ascend to Corporation Street again. After about fifty yards you will reach the buff terracotta and red brick **Pitman Building (28)** dating from 1897. At first floor level there is a series of lively reliefs representing carpenters and diners – a somewhat unlikely combination which acknowledges the original occupancy of the building by a distinguished furniture maker, A R Dean (whose name you will see above the entrance to No. 153A), and by a vegetarian restaurant. You will also see reliefs of the city coat of arms and, on the skyline, a group of three figures seemingly giving you a cheery welcome (though you will see this better after you have crossed to the other side of the road a little further ahead).

On the other side of the road is the Gazette Buildings, the former home of the Birmingham Gazette and then, on the corner of James Watt Street, the **Crown Inn (29).** As you will see, if you look up to the second floor inscription, this once also housed the Lincoln's Inn Restaurant – an indication that you are here in lawyer's territory.

Mural in Old Square

Following Pitman Building is the old County Court dating from 1882, now replaced by new courts in James Watt Street completed in 1987. Then, across Newton Street, are the **Victoria Law Courts (30).** The foundation stone was laid by Queen Victoria in 1887, the Jubilee year of her reign, and the building was completed in 1891. It is constructed externally in red terracotta and internally in pink and buff terracotta, a style that became very popular in Birmingham at this time. Terracotta is a type of hard brick which can be moulded and easily cleaned – an advantage in the grimy atmosphere of the Victorian city. The architects were Sir Aston Webb and Ingress Bell. Webb considered it his finest work and described its principal features as resembling those of the French style of Francis I.

Over the entrance there is an imposing statue of Queen Victoria and there are many other figures and much intricate decoration. An arched porch leads into a magnificent great hall with stained glass windows depicting Birmingham's trades, personalities and history, and with a fine timber framed roof. Around one of the internal balconies is the injunction 'Thou shalt not bear false witness against thy neighbour'. One hopes that this is always scrupulously observed!

The Birmingham Daily Post was highly enthusiastic about the new Victoria Law Courts and wrote, in 1889, 'The interesting windows, with their Gothic arches of buff terracotta afford a series of delightful cathedral-like vistas, and a nearer view of the ornamentation of the arches and capitals is an artistic treat' – doubtless this is a treat that many who

The Victoria Law Courts in 1891 Birmingham Public Libraries

have found themselves here would have willingly foregone!

Now retrace your steps to the pedestrian crossing, go over to the other side and continue forward along Corporation Street, remembering to look back to the figures above Pitman Building. About fifty yards along you will reach the **Methodist Central Hall (31).** This lively red brick and terracotta building, with a fine slender tower, was built in 1903-1904 and nicely complements the Victoria Law Courts and the Ruskin Buildings opposite. The entrance contains two interesting terracotta reliefs. One shows John Wesley preaching; the other an incident from his boyhood when he was rescued from his burning home, an event that some of his followers came to regard as miraculous. Methodism was brought to Birmingham by the Wesleys, not without risk. Charles Wesley, attempting to preach in the Bull Ring in 1746, was met with a barrage of stones, and John Wesley was in some peril when preaching in nearby Gosta Green

Queen Victoria above the entrance to the Law Courts

in 1747. However, Methodism eventually became accepted, and in 1783 a Methodist chapel was opened in Cherry Street, and this remained until it was demolished under Chamberlain's Corporation Street scheme.

Looking ahead beyond Corporation Street to Gosta Green you can see the **Central Fire Station (32),** surmounted by a clock and built in 1935. The Municipal Fire Brigade was established in 1875 and the first Central Fire Station was opened in 1883: before then the prime responsibility for fire services had been in the hands of insurance companies. Behind the fire station is the main building of Aston University.

Continue along Corporation Street which now curves sharply round to the left. On the other side of the road is a wine bar, an interesting feature of which is the bar counter which was constructed from the altar screen taken from the Church of the Messiah in Broad Street, demolished in 1978.

Walk along the pavement until at the road junction you reach some steps on your right. From this point you can look across to the **General Hospital (33)** in Steelhouse Lane. The first Birmingham General Hospital was built in Summer Lane at the suggestion of Dr John Ash who arranged a public meeting in 1765 to consider the project and to appeal for donations. Work started in 1766 but funds soon ran out and in 1768 a musical concert was held to raise more funds. This proved to be the forerunner of a great series of Birmingham triennial music festivals which continued until 1912 to raise money for the hospital. The hospital was opened in 1779 but although it was enlarged from time to time it was unable to keep up with the growing needs of the town. Eventually, in 1897, a new building in Steelhouse Lane, designed in keeping with the most up-to-date medical ideas of the time, was opened by Princess Christian of Schleswig Holstein (born Princess Helena), the third daughter of Queen Victoria. This was constructed in terracotta in Flemish Renaissance style. It was, in fact, the largest terracotta building in the city centre but, unfortunately, subsequent alterations and additions have severely distorted the original concept.

The name Steelhouse Lane is derived, as a map of 1731 shows, from the eighteenth century "Kettle's Steel Houses". These were furnaces for converting iron into steel which was becoming popular for ornamental objects. This same map also records that in 1731 the population of Birmingham was 23,286. Today it is just over a million although, of course, the boundaries of the city are much wider than in earlier times. The original area of the township of Birmingham was just under 3,000 acres; today it is over 65,000 acres. The expansion has taken in many ancient parishes, some of which were at one time much more important than Birmingham itself. One such is Aston which was incorporated into the city in 1903 and which you are now about to enter.

Now walk down the steps on the right, turn right and then left to pass under the James Watt section of the Queensway. The Queensway is the ring road around the city centre, constructed between 1957 and 1970 and opened by HM the Queen in April 1971. The Queensway was originally intended to be known simply as the Ringway, and Queensway was to be just one section of it. However, due to some administrative slip, the Queen was not told and she gave the name to the whole of the road!

One of the five stone crosses on the campus of Aston University

City Coat of Arms from original council housing in Ryder Street, now on the Vauxhall Dining Centre

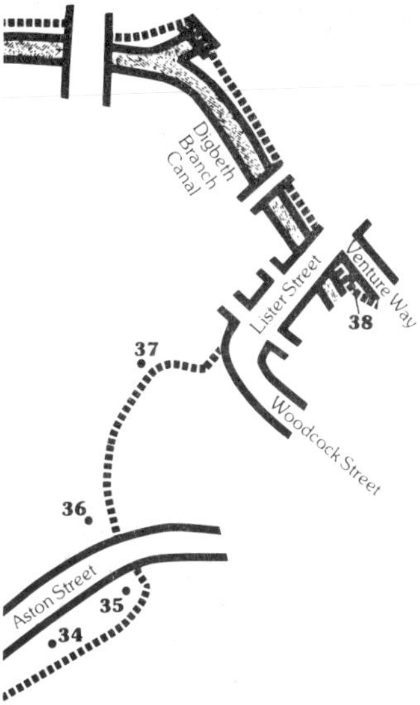

The Queensway channels cross-city traffic away from the centre which is now a quieter and cleaner place.

As you emerge from the underpass walk up the steps facing and you will find yourself in the campus of Aston University, Birmingham's second university. The University had its origins in the Municipal Technical School (subsequently the Central Technical College) opened in 1895. The College, which become the Birmingham College of Advanced Technology in 1956, moved from its old site in Suffolk Street to the present site in the 1950s and received its royal charter as a university in 1966. This area is known now as the Aston Triangle. It was originally an open common covered with grass and gorse, hence its older and better known name of Gosta Green (from Gorsty Green, by which it was known in the seventeenth century).

Immediately on your left you will see one of the tower block student residences, Stafford Tower. A little further on you come to the **Vauxhall Dining Centre (34)** – the Birmingham Coat of Arms on the front of this comes from one of the old houses, now demolished, which stood nearby in Ryder Street. In the 1880s the Council was criticised for the fact that although it had spent approaching two million pounds on the Corporation Street scheme it had done nothing to provide desperately needed houses for working people. Eventually, in 1889, twenty-two two-storey cottages were built in what became Ryder Street, another eighty-two being erected in 1891. These were let for 5s 6d (27.5p) per week, the Council providing a subsidy of 1s 3d (6.25p) per week. This was the first municipal housing to be constructed in the city. Ryder Street has now disappeared, the area today forming part of the Aston campus.

A few yards further on is the **Gem Sports Hall (35)** – the interesting configuration of one wall is not some modern abstract design but a 'climbing wall' on which students can learn the techniques of rock climbing. Close by you will see a stone cross, the central one of five on the campus. These are laid out in the form of a Southern Cross and although they are all different they have a common structural basis. They are intended to provide a unifying feature on the campus.

Now turn sharp left around the Sports Hall and walk forward to Aston Street. On the way you will pass two more stone crosses. Facing you on the other side of Aston Street is the **main university building (36)** opened by HM the Queen in 1955, the foundation stone having been laid by Princess Margaret in 1951. The somewhat forbidding appearance of this building has been improved by the recent addition of a glass entrance hall and a pair of panoramic lifts. The section of Aston Street to your left has also been attractively landscaped.

Cross Aston Street and turn right to walk past the main building. Next on your left you will see the Guild of Students building and, to the right of this and some yards back, a Victorian drinking fountain. Ahead is **The Studio (37),**now part of the University's Arts Centre but originally the Delicia Picture House, one of Birmingham's early cinemas, opened in 1924. After the cinema closed it became the BBC's Midland Television Centre and was then acquired by the University when the BBC left for the new Pebble Mill Centre.

Turn right in front of The Studio and then left by the Sacks of Potatoes, a pleasant public house dating from 1828. Over to your right you can see the University's Management Centre. Go down Lister Street to the bridge over the canal. The lively modern buildings along the towpath to the right form part of the **Aston Science Park (38),** a city enterprise developed in association with the University and Lloyds Bank. The Science Park provides accommodation for companies involved in the field of modern technology who can obtain support from the research facilities and the technological expertise of the university.

Cross to the right-hand side of the road, turn right along Venture Way and then right again between the two Science Park buildings. This will take you on to the towpath of part of the complex of canals known as the Birmingham Canal Navigations (BCN). The BCN was

The Sacks of Potatoes on the Aston Campus

The Aston Science Park

formed in 1784 by the amalgamation of two canal companies, the Birmingham Canal Company and the Birmingham and Fazeley Canal Company. The original name of the combined company was the 'Birmingham and Birmingham and Fazeley Canal Company' but this fearsome title was changed to Birmingham Canal Navigations in 1794. Subsequently, other companies were acquired and by 1865 the Company owned some 160 miles of canals, about 100 miles of which remain.

The canals first came to Birmingham in 1768 when James Brindley was authorised to build the Birmingham Canal from Birmingham to meet the Staffordshire and Worcestershire Canal north of Wolverhampton. This section, known as the Digbeth Branch, links together the Birmingham and Fazeley Canal, opened in 1789, and a part of the Grand Union Canal which was opened in 1844. The canals, which have been described as 'the arteries of the Industrial Revolution', had a dramatic effect on the economy of the region and contributed greatly to Birmingham's prosperity. For example, when the first boat load of coal arrived in Birmingham in 1769 the price of coal was halved immediately. The poet, John Freeth, celebrated the arrival of the first coal boats thus:

> Then revel in gladness, let harmony flow,
> From the district of Bordesley to Paradise Row;
> For true feeling in each breast must be wrought,
> When coals under fivepence per hundred are bought.

You are now on a section of towpath which has been imaginatively

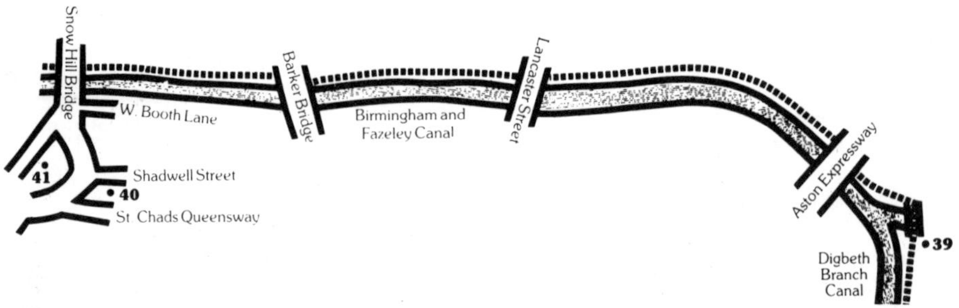

renovated by the West Midlands County Council. Turn right along this towpath, passing under Lister Street bridge. The next bridge, under Love Lane, carries an attractive spiral staircase: beyond you will see a recently landscaped area to your left. Very soon you will reach **Aston Junction (39)** where the present canal joins the Birmingham and Fazeley Canal. Turn right to the attractive brick bridge from where the flight of eleven Aston locks takes the canal down to Salford Junction, an important canal junction which now lies below the Gravelly Hill motorway interchange (Spaghetti Junction). Cross the bridge and turn left, passing under a fine cast-iron bridge inscribed 'Horseley Iron Works, Staffordshire, 1828'. The next bridge takes you under the end of the Aston Expressway, the motorway link between the city and the M6.

You are now heading back into the city centre. On your way you will cross several bridges which originally took the

Approaching the Birmingham Radio Tower along the Birmingham & Fazeley Canal

towpath over canal links into nearby factories, a reminder of the vital importance that the canals once had to local industry. In 1839 it was recorded that there were "about 124 Wharfs and Works ... seated on the Banks of the Canals, between Farmer's Bridge and Aston". The ribbed brickwork underfoot on the bridges, mostly recently restored by the County Council, is of the traditional pattern so designed to prevent the horses which drew the canal boats from slipping. Ahead you will soon see the Birmingham Radio Tower, 150 metres high and formerly known as the Post Office Tower. This is a main link in British Telecom's ultra high frequency television and telephone network and is able to deal simultaneously with 150,000 telephone and seventy television channels.

The next bridge takes you under Lancaster Street. The red doors in this bridge provide access to water for the Fire Service. You will see a number of these as you walk along the canal: they were installed in the Second World War as a precaution against the mains supply being lost by bombing. As you leave the bridge look back up at it and you will see the decorated back of a Victorian cast-iron urinal, several of which can still be found around Birmingham.

After passing under Barker Bridge, built in 1842, there is a good view to the left of some of the modern buildings in the city centre. You can also see the twin spires of **St. Chad's Cathedral (40).** This is Birmingham's Roman Catholic cathedral, built between 1839 and 1841, and the first post-Reformation Roman Catholic cathedral to be erected in Britain. It is quite plain, in fourteenth century German style, and is constructed from red brick and Welsh slate. It is the work of Augustus Pugin,

St. Chad's Cathedral from the Kennedy Gardens

better known as the designer of much of the decorative architecture of the Houses of Parliament. The materials for the construction of the cathedral were brought along the canal, a branch line (no longer in existence) originally extending into this area.

At this point it is worth making a detour from the main route of the walk to visit St. Chad's and the nearby Kennedy Gardens. (IF YOU WISH TO OMIT THIS SECTION OF THE WALK NOW TURN TO p36.) For the detour leave the canal by the gate on the right just before the next bridge, Snow Hill Bridge. Turn left when you emerge to the road, cross the canal and William Booth Lane (leading to the Social Service Centre of the Salvation Army, founded by William Booth) and descend the steps ahead. Then go through the second tunnel on your right (Shadwell Subway) which will bring you to a ramp. Ascend this and bear left to reach the Cathedral entrance. The interior is spacious and very attractive, in particular the painted roof and the stained glass windows which were made locally in Hardman's Studios. One set of these, on the north wall, illustrates the making of the windows and includes pictures of John Hardman (dressed in red). The windows in the St.Edward Chapel (to the left) tell the story of the relics of St. Chad, Bishop of Mercia, who died in 672. A thigh bone of St. Chad can be seen in this chapel and other relics of St. Chad are contained in a gilt casket above the high altar.

In the Lady Chapel (to the left of the chancel) can be seen the 'halfpenny window', paid for by halfpenny donations by the children of St. Chad's school and installed in 1844.

The impressive pulpit was made in Brabant early in the 1500s and came from the Abbey of St. Gertrude, Louvain. The carvings in the pulpit are of four of the fathers of the church – from left to right, St. Jerome, St. Gregory the Great, St. Augustin of Hippo and St. Ambrose.

The cathedral contains some fifteenth century German material including pieces of carvings in the chancel stalls. There is a carving on the back of the Provost's Chair (in the chancel, to the left) which, together with those in the stalls, came from the church of St. Mary in Capitolio in Cologne. The statue of the Virgin Mary in the Lady Chapel is also a fifteenth century German work although the paint-work is by Pugin. It was presented to the Cathedral by Pugin.

On the underside of the seats of the chancel stalls are some delightful carvings showing peasants, leaves, an owl, a lion, a griffin and a swan.

St. Chad's stands in what was originally the gun making area of the city. The manufacture of guns began in Birmingham in the sixteenth or seventeenth century. The trade was certainly well established in the 1690s when 200 muskets a month were being supplied to the Government. During the Napoleonic Wars two-thirds of the

The pulpit in St. Chad's

Birmingham Public Libraries

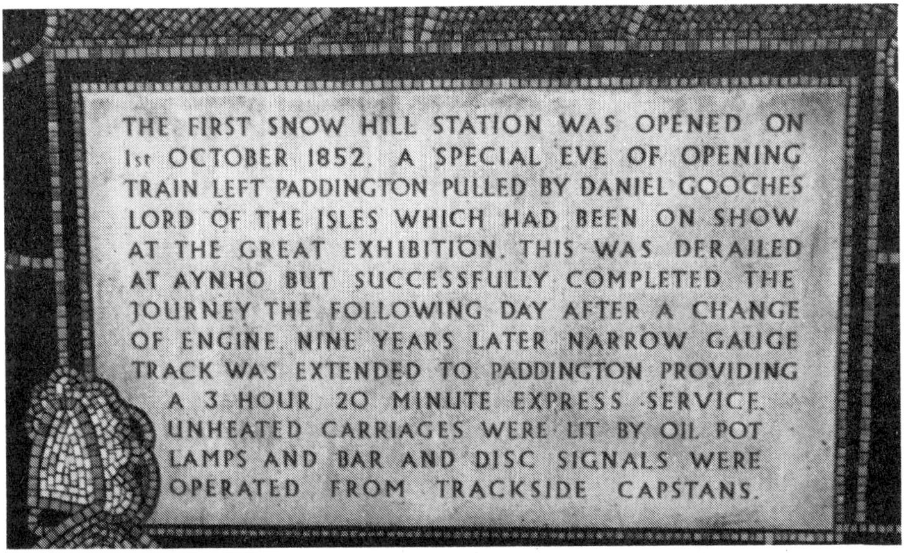

Part of the GWR mural in the Kennedy Gardens

British fire-arms came from Birmingham, as well as swords for the army and cutlasses for the navy. In 1813 an Act of Parliament, sponsored by Birmingham's major arms manufacturers, authorised the building of the Birmingham Proof House in which guns could be proofed (tested). Between 1855 and 1864 some six million weapons were tested here, about 70% having been made in Birmingham. This impressive building still stands in Banbury Street, close to the canal. Although not on the route of this walk it can easily be seen by rail travellers shortly after leaving New Street station on the line to Coventry and Euston.

One important gun maker was Samuel Galton. He was a member of the Lunar Society, founded in 1766, a meeting ground for notable scientists and philosophers. Its membership included such famous names as Erasmus Darwin, Matthew Boulton, James Watt, William Murdoch, John Baskerville and Joseph Priestley. The society took its name from the practice of the members of meeting on the Monday nearest to the full moon, thereby being provided with light for their journey home. At this time, of course, public lighting of the streets was almost non-existent.

On leaving the Cathedral retrace your steps for a few yards, but then, instead of descending the ramp go down the steps to the left, through the tunnel on your left (St. Chad's Subway) and then the tunnel on the right (Kennedy Subway). This will take you into **Kennedy Gardens (41).** Here is a memorial to the late President John Kennedy and also a superb set of mosaics and plaques, 300 feet long and 17 feet high, telling the story of the Great Western Railway. After walking round the gardens retrace your steps to the canal, noting, as you approach it, the impressive Victorian Gothic building in red terracotta on the corner of Hampton Street and Constitution Hill.

RESUME FROM HERE IF YOU HAVE OMITTED THE VISIT TO ST CHAD'S.

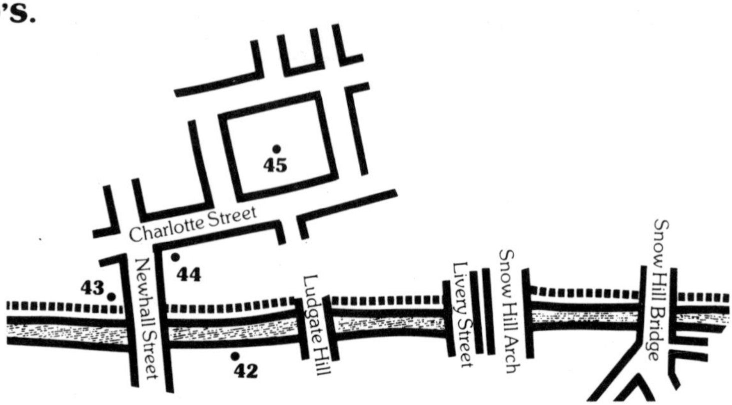

Continuing the main route along the canal, Snow Hill Bridge brings you to the first of the thirteen Farmer's Bridge locks which take the Birmingham and Fazeley Canal to its junction with the Birmingham Canal. Birmingham is on a sandstone ridge so all the canals into Birmingham go uphill. This necessitates a good supply of water from reservoirs, the most important being the Edgbaston reservoir.

Next comes one of the massive arches of the old Snow Hill station built by Brunel in the 1850s, followed by a narrow cramped bridge under Livery Street. After passing under the Ludgate Hill bridge the towpath runs close to the **Birmingham Radio Tower (42)** and reaches a section where building extends over the canal, a reflection of the high property values in this area.

Next, another narrow cramped bridge takes the canal under Newhall Street. Stairs immediately on the right (and easily missed!) then lead you up to the **Museum of Science and Industry (43)**. The site was originally occupied by Elkington's electro-plating factory dating from the 1840s, and one of the workshops has been retained as the Engineering Hall, an impressive gallery with an arched roof. The Museum was established in 1950 to preserve examples of engines and machine tools, and was soon extended to include industrial products, transport and technology. It also contains a Modern Science section. The Museum houses a unique record of Birmingham's industrial past and is well worth a visit.

On the opposite side of the street, bearing an impressive coat of arms, is the **Assay Office (44),** one of four such offices (the others are in London, Edinburgh and Sheffield) responsible for assaying (testing) and hallmarking articles made from gold, silver and platinum. The hallmarking system was originated by a statute of Edward I in the year 1300. The principal purpose of the system was the same then as it is today – the protection of the public against fraud and of the trader against unfair competition.

The manufacture of silver articles on a substantial scale began in Birmingham in the eighteenth century. In 1762 the industrialist Matthew Boulton opened a factory, the Soho Works, for the production of fine quality silverware in Handsworth, then just outside the northern boundary of Birmingham. At that time the nearest assay office was in Chester and sending all the goods there and back involved considerable expense, delay and possible damage. Consequently Boulton, supported by other local silversmiths, approached his neighbour Lord Dartmouth, a Secretary of State, who lived in Sandwell Park, West Bromwich. On Lord Dartmouth's advice an Act of Parliament was promoted to authorise an assay office in Birmingham, an Act that was supported by local nobility and gentry, some of whom were land-owners and were therefore interested in industrial developments that would add to property values. In spite of opposition from the London assay office a Bill to establish offices in Birmingham and Sheffield was eventually passed in 1773.

The first Birmingham office occupied three rooms in an inn in New Street. However, as Birmingham's industrial activity expanded, the work of the assay office grew and in 1790 it acquired offices of its own, moving into the present premises in 1877. Today the office hallmarks some eight million articles a year.

IF YOU WANT TO OMIT THE NEXT SECTION OF THE WALK (TO ST. PAUL'S SQUARE) TURN NOW TO PAGE 40.

Turn right by the side of the Assay Office and walk along Charlotte Street to **St. Paul's Square (45),** the last remaining eighteenth century square in Birmingham. Central to this is St. Paul's church which was consecrated in 1779 on land given by the Colmore family.

An exhibit from the Museum of Science & Industry Birmingham Museum & Art Gallery

The spire was added in 1823: the plan for this, dated 6 August 1822, can be seen in the gallery.

St. Paul's has many similarities in appearance to St. Martin-in-the-Fields in London. It was the church in which Matthew Boulton and James Watt worshipped. Most of the original boxed pews with their fine numberplates remain unchanged from when the church was built.

The east window contains some attractive painted (not stained) glass by Francis Eginton and depicts three scenes from the life of St. Paul, the centrepiece being *The Conversion of St. Paul.*

The south-east window commemorates William Hollins, a local sculptor, and his family. The sculptured marble surround contains a bust of Hollins with his family named on 'the fruitful vine' and 'the olive plant', a reference to Psalm 128. It was made by William's son Peter. Several monuments in the church are the work of William.

St. Paul's has superb acoustics and a long tradition of music making. Concerts were held to pay for Thomas Eginton's window but they were not profitable and he never received his money! Concerts are held regularly here today, some being broadcast by the BBC. The fine organ was rebuilt in 1965.

The square was originally a residential area for wealthy business people, many of whom were concerned with the

St. Paul's Square

manufacture of jewellery which became centred in this area. However, by about the middle of the nineteenth century many houses had been converted into workshops and the area around St. Paul's had become Birmingham's jewellery quarter. The discovery of gold in quantity in Africa, America and Australia (1849 was the date of the California Gold Rush), and the increasing living standards of working people, led to a massive demand for cheap jewellery and trinkets. The development of electro-plating gave an additional boost to the trade, and the manufacture of plated jewellery and toys became one of the chief activities of local craftsmen. It was said at the time

> 'All that is needed for a workman to start as a master is a bench and a leather apron, one or two pounds worth of tools, and for material, a few sovereigns and some ounces of copper and zinc . . .'

After walking around the square return to the canal, noting as you reach Newhall Street the attractive frontage of the Queen's Arms public house dating from the early 1900s. Overlooking the canal is Canning Walk, part of the recent canalside development.

Canning Walk and the Birmingham & Fazeley Canal

RESUME FROM HERE IF YOU HAVE OMITTED THE VISIT TO ST. PAUL'S.

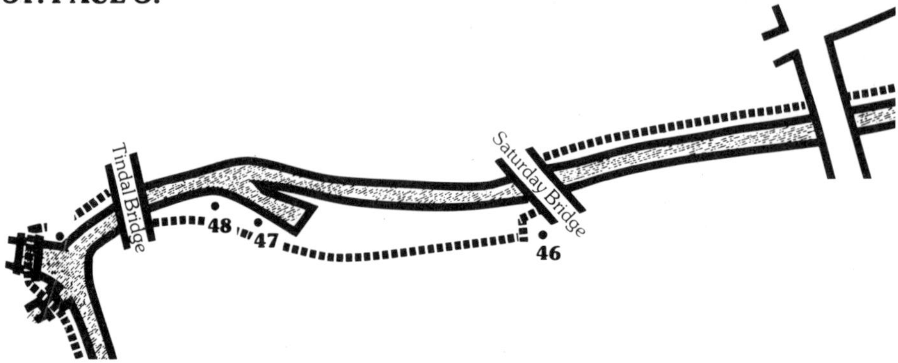

Return down the steps when, continuing along the canal, and after more locks, you will reach the Saturday Bridge where the canal passes under Summer Row. A short way along Summer Row a 'Friday Bridge' used to carry the road over the Newhall Branch of the canal – long since filled in and built over. It is thought that these quaint names result from the canal company's practice of paying some canal workers each Friday at the Friday Bridge and the remainder the next day at the Saturday Bridge. Go under the Saturday Bridge, turn up to the road and cross the bridge, looking ahead for a good view of 'Big Brum'. Now continue along the left-hand side of the canal. You are here on **James Brindley Walk (46),** part of a canalside development which gained for Birmingham a Civic Trust award 'for creating an environment of great character and delightful charm which makes an outstanding contribution to the amenities of the city'. After about 20 yards take the steps on your left and continue forward along the Walk. Just past a garden on your right you will see two plaques set into a brick base. One of these includes a map of the Birmingham canals, the other records the opening of the walk:

Old crane at The Long Boat

James Brindley Walk.

This plaque commemorates the opening of James Brindley Walk and was unveiled by the Lord Mayor Ald. N B A Bosworth Ll B on Saturday 26th June 1969.

The canalside walk stands on the site of the Newhall Branch, part of the original Birmingham Canal built by James Brindley in 1769.

This canal laid the foundations of the Birmingham Canal Navigations and contributed significantly to the commercial prosperity of Birmingham.

1769-1969

Continue forward passing, on your left, an old crane (not originally on this site but brought in for decorative purposes) and, on your right, the canal basin. Further over, beyond the basin, is the highest of the Farmer's Bridge locks. If you look across to this you will see nearby an old toll office, a reminder of the times when tolls had to be paid based on the weight and the nature of the goods carried. You are now at Cambrian Wharf and ahead you can see the **Long Boat (47),** a modern pub with, inside, a fine collection of canal memorabilia.

Go behind the Long Boat and up a slope, with at its upper end some well-worn original stone paving, that takes you from the Wharf to Kingston Row. Ahead you will see some attractive **eighteenth century cottages (48)** modernised in 1969 as part of the canal-side development scheme . Turn right for a view over the canal at a point where Farmer's Bridge (from which the

Canalside cottages in Kingston Row

Plaque at Cambrian Wharf

flight of thirteen locks gets its name) used to cross the canal. Farmer's Bridge has no agricultural connotations – it simply led to some property belonging to a Mr Farmer! Now go back and around the cottages to a pleasant grassed and seated area overlooking the canal. From here cross Tindal Bridge and return to the towpath.

Now continue forward under Tindal Bridge and then another Horseley Iron Works bridge dated 1827. You are now at **Farmer's Bridge junction (49)** where the Birmingham canal and the Birmingham and Fazeley canals meet. Just near here the canal passes over the Ladywood Tunnel built by Robert Stephenson in 1846-7 as part of the original Stour Valley Railway. It carries trains on the Birmingham to Wolverhampton line.

On an island at the junction is a signpost giving directions to Wolverhampton (13 miles, 3 locks), Fazeley (15 miles, 38 locks) and Worcester (30 miles, 58 locks). Carry on past the signpost, turn left over the next iron bridge, then left again and continue forward over another bridge. Beneath this runs the original line of Brindley's Birmingham Canal. When this was constructed, between 1767 and 1769, it followed a twisting route, keeping as far as possible to a natural contour to avoid the necessity for cuttings, and to take water from the nearby brooks. However, the many bends created difficulties for the boats and in 1824 Thomas Telford was engaged to construct a straightened line to Wolverhampton. One loop bypassed by Telford's work is the Sheepcote Street loop, one end of which you are now passing over.

The canal now bends right to reach the Broad Street tunnel. As you walk through this you can see that it has been extended several times. When you emerge you are at the Worcester Bar Basin, more commonly known as **Gas Street Basin (50).** This is the hub of the extensive network of West Midlands canals which, although much developed in recent years, still retains some of its old atmosphere. A few of the old buildings remain, and there are

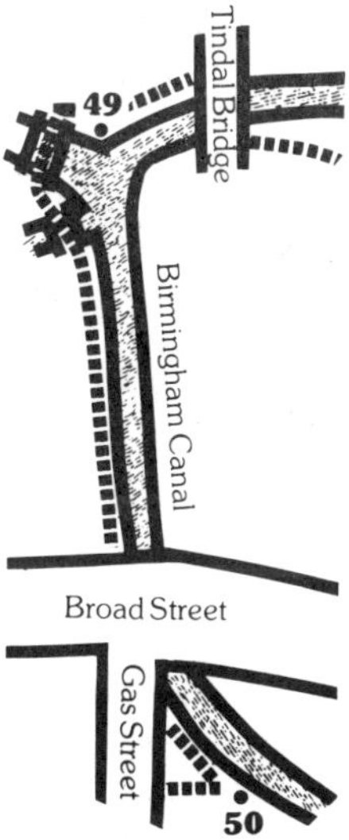

A quiet canalside garden near Tindal Bridge

Traditional boats and modern buildings at Gas Street Basin

many gaily decorated narrow boats. Across on the opposite side of the basin the modern development includes an attractive pub, appropriately named the James Brindley, to which a recently constructed bridge provides access.

Ahead is the Worcester and Birmingham canal built between 1791 and 1815. This was originally separated from the Birmingham canal by a narrow strip of land and goods had to be carried across here from the one canal to the other. This unsatisfactory situation, although of financial benefit to the powerful Birmingham Canal Company, was eventually resolved by an Act of Parliament in 1815. As a result of this Act, the bar was replaced by a stop lock, the remains of which you can see beside the bridge. A stop lock simply controls the flow of water between one canal and another. Water supply was always a problem on the canals and companies had no wish to provide a free supply to their competitors.

Walk up the slope to the right into Gas Street, so named because the premises of the Birmingham Gas Company were once nearby. Street lighting first came to Birmingham in 1818, supplied from the gasworks of a Mr J Gostling who had installed gas lighting in Parliament Street, Westminster, and who subsequently established the Birmingham Gas Company. The company was acquired by the Corporation in 1875.

Here you will leave the peace of the canals behind you and soon find yourself back among the bustle of the busy city. Turn right and walk along Gas Street which will bring you to Broad Street: cross this by the pedestrian crossing, noting as you reach the other side the old **Birmingham Brass House (51),** built in 1781. The central

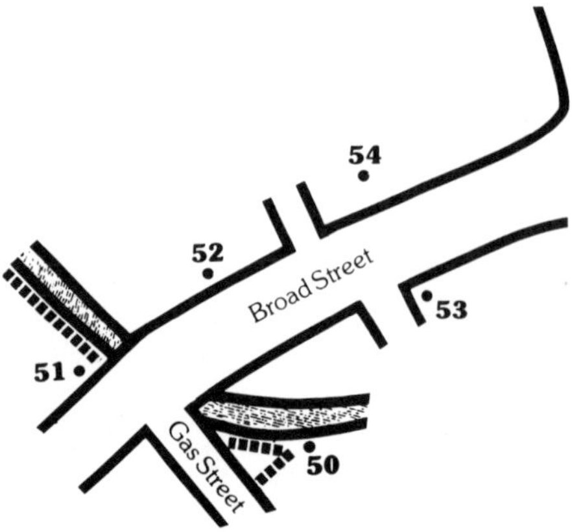

doorway, flanked by granite columns, was added in the 1870s and replaced a carriageway which went through the building. With the construction of the nearby canal a number of brass foundries sprang up alongside and by the end of the eighteenth century brass was one of Birmingham's important manufactures.

Turn right to walk along Broad Street. This area is now covered by the Broad Street development plan which will establish here Birmingham's new International Conference Centre, work on which commenced in 1986 and which is scheduled for completion in 1990. The development is funded jointly by the city and the EEC. When complete it will contain a number of conference and exhibition halls, and a new concert hall seating 2,200.

A little way along is **The Crown (52),** built in 1781 but altered several times since. In the nineteenth century the club room of The Crown was an important centre for political meetings. An attractive feature of the building is the clock surmounted by a green copper cupola. Inside, in the lounge, are several interesting oil paintings, including one showing the inn in 1781. William Butler, a founder of the Birmingham brewery

Boulton, Murdoch and Watt

firm of Mitchells and Butlers, came to Birmingham at the age of 16 in 1859. He took a job with a hairdresser in Deritend and, in his spare time, worked behind the bar at The Crown. He soon decided that his future lay in the licensed trade and he became the licensee of the London Works Tavern in Smethwick. In 1876 he acquired The Crown and soon built a large brewery, with a capacity of 5,000 barrels a week, on the site. In 1898 William Butler entered into partnership with a Smethwick brewer, Henry Mitchell, and brewing operations were then concentrated in Mitchell's brewery in Cape Hill.

On the other side of Broad Street you will see **Birmingham Register Office (53),** the forecourt of which is often, and especially on Saturdays, thronged with wedding parties. (This building may be demolished as part of the Broad Street development). In the forecourt are fine gilded statues by William Bloye, a noted Birmingham sculptor. They were unveiled in 1956 and are to three great pioneers of the Industrial Revolution, Boulton, Watt and Murdoch. Matthew Boulton (some of whose silverware you may have seen in the Museum and Art Gallery) originally used water as a source of power for his Soho Works. However, finding this inadequate for his needs, he engaged the Scottish engineer, James Watt, to develop a more efficient, steam powered, engine. It proved highly successful and a variety of steam engines were then added to the Soho Works' range of products, many being exported around the world.

Another Scot, William Murdoch, invented gas lighting which enabled the Soho Works to be lit at night and twenty-four hour production maintained. Gas fittings then became another important product of the Soho Works.

Now, set back from the road, you will see on your left the **Repertory Theatre (54).** The first repertory theatre in Birmingham was in Station Street (near to New Street station) and which opened in 1913 with a performance of Twelfth Night. It had been built at his own expense, and was subsidised for many years, by Sir Barry Jackson who eventually established the theatre's world wide reputation. The original building still exists, and continues in use as a theatre, but the Repertory Theatre moved to the new

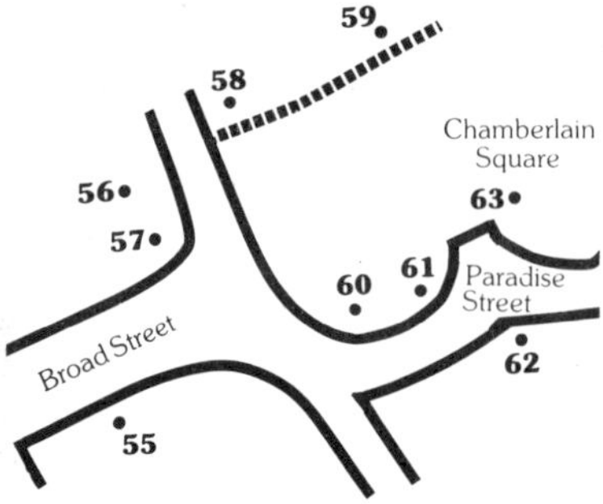

premises in 1971. It was the second new theatre to be opened in Birmingham within a decade, the nearby Crescent Theatre having been opened in 1964. In the foyer there is a bust of Sir Barry Jackson and a plaque with the inscription

> He poured his fortune and his talent into the Theatre with no thought of gain, taking nothing from it except some quiet satisfaction in the knowledge that the Drama in every aspect had been faithfully served.

On the ground floor, within the curved glass frontage, is the restaurant, the entrance to the theatre being on the right. The exterior is faced with white rough textured concrete pre-cast panels – showing that this building medium, when used imaginatively, can present

Birmingham Repertory Theatre

an elegant appearance which nicely blends with the neighbouring stone buildings.

Looking across Broad Street you will see, to the left of the Register Office, two buildings dating from the 1930s. The **Trustee Savings Bank (55),** of Ionic Neoclassical design, originally housed the Birmingham Municipal Bank. This was established in 1916 by the city under the Lord Mayor, Neville Chamberlain, son of Joseph and future Prime Minister. Originally intended simply to help the war effort by promoting war savings it proved so successful that it was fully established by Act of Parliament in 1919. The foundation stone of the present building was laid by Neville Chamberlain, then Chancellor of the Exchequer, on 22 October 1932, and the building was opened by Prince George on 27 November 1933. The Municipal Bank has now lost its independence and is part of the Trustee Savings Bank.

Next to the Bank is the headquarters of Central Independent Television. This was originally built as a Masonic Temple for the Freemasons of Warwickshire as evidenced by the fine masonic frieze along the north elevation. The Freemasons lost the building at the outbreak of war in 1939 when it was requisitioned at seven days notice for use by the Ministry of Food. The central doorway was originally flanked by two Ionic columns but these were removed in the early 1960s when it became The Engineering and Building Centre. It was acquired by Alpha Television, the predecessor of Central, in the late

Baskerville House

1970s. It is connected at the rear by a linking bridge to four studios, the whole site occupying about an acre and providing employment for some 900 staff. Towering high above is the tall and elegant Alpha Tower, an office block set in a particularly attractive modern square. If you want to make a short detour to see this you can reach it via the underpass a little further ahead.

On your left is a pleasant formal garden behind which is **Baskerville House (56),** named after John Baskerville who was born at Wolverley, near Kidderminster, in 1706. Baskerville was a highly successful manufacturer of japanned (lacquered) metal goods who, in the middle of the eighteenth century, turned to printing and type designing, becoming printer to the University of Cambridge. He laid the foundations of Birmingham's important printing industry and established the town as a centre of the printing art. The Birmingham School of Printing is still prominent in this field.

Baskerville lived in a mansion in Broad Street called Easy Hill on the site of Baskerville House. When this was sold in 1788 the advertisement ran

> 'the estate consists of about seven acres of rich Pasture Land in high condition, Part of which is laid out in Shady Walks, adorned with Shrubberies, Fish Ponds and a Grotto.'

You will search in vain for these today!

Baskerville House was constructed in 1939, and was intended to be the first of three blocks to be placed around a formal garden and to be known as the Civic Centre. However, the war intervened and plans for the remaining two buildings were then abandoned. If you look back across to the Trustee Savings Bank you will see that the Bank and Baskerville House are in very similar style: they were designed by the same architect, Cecil Howett.

The foundation stone for Baskerville House was laid by the Lord Mayor in June 1938. This was in the middle of Birmingham's centenary year for it was in 1838 that the municipal charter was granted which established representative local government. The council had fewer powers then than it subsequently acquired, its main function being the control of the police. The government of the day was reluctant to allow too much power to local authorities fearing that the councils might become too political – a fear that seemingly still haunts Whitehall today!

At the end of the garden is one of Birmingham's best known buildings, the **Hall of Memory (57).** The

The Hall of Memory

foundation stone for this was laid by the Prince of Wales on 12 June 1923 and it was opened in 1925. Like the surrounding buildings it is constructed from Portland stone. It is octagonal in shape and has four bronze statues outside representing the armed services. Inside there are interesting carvings on the wall, a fine stained glass window of geometric design, and a book of remembrance on a carved marble plinth. Its modest style is a refreshing change from many of the war memorials that were erected in Britain at this time.

Facing you across the Queensway is, on the left, the glass fronted **Copthorne Hotel (58)** and, on the right, the matching Chamberlain House, built in 1986/7. Go under the Queensway by the underpass ahead and carry on forward between the hotel and Chamberlain House to the **Central Library (59),** passing on your left the Grapevine public house.

The Central Library, opened in 1973, is one of the largest libraries in Europe and holds over a million books housed on nine floors. It is on the site of Josiah Mason's Science College which was built in 1875 and demolished in 1963. As is recorded by a plaque on the library, Josiah Mason was a carpet weaver's son from Kidderminster who prospered by the manufacture of split rings and steel pens. He gave the city an orphanage for poor children and these children were given preference for admission to the college. Mason College became the University of Birmingham in 1900, Joseph Chamberlain and the Editor of the

Birmingham Central Library

Birmingham Post having campaigned hard for this and raised funds locally. Birmingham University is today one of Britain's major universities and is now located in the Edgbaston district of the city.

In the complex of buildings of which the Library forms part is the **Shakespeare Memorial Room (60).** This has its origins in the Shakespeare Library which was formed in 1864, the tercentenary of Shakespeare's birth. The collection was housed in the Central Library in a room designed by J H Chamberlain (whose School of Art and Crafts was seen earlier in Margaret Street). The design of the room, in Elizabethan style, was highly praised at the time. When the Central Library was demolished in 1974 the wooden bookcases were dismantled and then re-erected in the present room in 1985, the original joiner's marks being used to guide the restorers. The plasterwork ceiling, which had been destroyed, was re-created from fragments of the original and from photographs. Stained glass was made in imitation of the original.

The Shakespeare Library itself now comprises some 42,000 books and a vast collection of illustrations and is housed on the sixth floor of the Central Library. The material in the Shakespeare Memorial Room is mainly made up of duplicates donated by Wigan and Westminster Public libraries, but also contains various memorabilia from the original Library.

Entrance to Queen's College

James Watt

Adjacent to the Shakespeare Room are the Library Exhibition Hall, in which periodic book and other exhibitions are held, and the Adrian Boult Hall, a superb new concert hall opened in 1986 by the Queen Mother and forming part of the nearby **Birmingham School of Music (61).** The School of Music was established in 1886, originally as part of the Birmingham and Midland Institute, and is now a part of Birmingham Polytechnic. Its first Principal was Sir Granville Bantock. The School has always played a notable part in Birmingham's musical activities.

The Central Library faces a piazza, Chamberlain Square, which incorporates a gracefully curved stepped area leading down to the Town Hall and the Council House. It contains statues of Priestley and Watt. Dr Joseph Priestley was an eminent philosopher and scientist who came to Birmingham in 1780 as minister of the Unitarian New Meeting House chapel. He was the discoverer of oxygen, nitrogen, ammonia and other chemical substances and conducted many scientific experiments in the private laboratory at his home in nearby Sparkbrook. However, this was a time when revolution was in the air. In July 1791 Priestley's chapel, home and his records of a quarter of a century of scientific work were destroyed in three days of rioting. Shortly afterwards, Priestley emigrated to the United States where he spent the rest of his life. The statue represents Priestley using a burning glass to heat mercuric oxide, an experiment which led to his discovery of oxygen.

If you stand beside the statue of Watt you can see, in Paradise Street, the **Queen's College building (62),** now the offices of a bank. Queen's College was chartered in 1843 and originally included departments of arts, science, medicine and theology. However, hopes that it would become the main centre of higher education in the Midlands never materialised and science and medicine were absorbed by Mason College in the 1880s. What remained became a theological college for the training of the clergy, and this moved to Edgbaston in 1920 where it still exists. The facade of the building was replaced around 1900 by the present Flemish Gothic pale terracotta. Indeed, this facade is all that remains of the college building, the interior having been completely rebuilt and converted into offices.

Now descend the steps to the **Chamberlain Memorial Fountain (63).** This memorial to Birmingham's most distinguished figure, with its Gothic gables and spires and incorporating a portrait medallion of Chamberlain, was constructed from Portland stone and erected in 1881, a year after Joseph Chamberlain had left local Government for a distinguished parliamentary career, becoming Colonial Secretary. It was restored to mark the Diamond Jubilee of the Birmingham Civic Society in 1978. The Civic Society was formed in 1918 for citizens 'who desire to stimulate a deeper concern in the beauty of their city, and a regard for the study and preservation of the best things of the past'.

The Chamberlain Memorial Fountain

Chamberlain medallion (above)
Chamberlain plaque (below)

This is a fitting point to end your tour of Birmingham, and if you wish to rest your limbs and have some refreshment you have at hand the Edwardian Tea Room in the Art Gallery, just a few yards away. But in this walk you have only covered a part of this fascinating city and there is much more to explore another day. To help you, the Birmingham Urban Studies Committee has produced a useful set of guides to various areas and aspects of Birmingham known as 'Brum Trails' which you will find on sale in the Art Gallery Shop and the Library Shop. Happy exploring!